Joseph Leidy, Romyn Hitchcock

Synopsis of the Fresh-Water Rhizopods

Joseph Leidy, Romyn Hitchcock

Synopsis of the Fresh-Water Rhizopods

ISBN/EAN: 9783337140762

Printed in Europe, USA, Canada, Australia, Japan

Cover: Foto ©ninafisch / pixelio.de

More available books at **www.hansebooks.com**

SYNOPSIS

OF THE

FRESH-WATER RHIZOPODS

A CONDENSED ACCOUNT

OF THE

GENERA AND SPECIES

FOUNDED UPON

PROF. JOSEPH LEIDY'S

"*FRESH-WATER RHIZOPODS OF NORTH AMERICA*"

COMPILED BY

ROMYN HITCHCOCK, F. R. M. S.

President of the New York Microscopical Society, Editor of the American
Monthly Microscopical Journal

NEW YORK

ROMYN HITCHCOCK, PUBLISHER

NOS. 51 AND 53 MAIDEN LANE

....

1881

INTRODUCTION.

It is sincerely hoped that the publication of this work will arouse an interest in the examination and study of the simple and beautiful organisms which it describes. It is seldom that a person can take up any study in natural history, and follow it in a satisfactory manner without access to many large and expensive books of reference. Until the publication of Professor Joseph Leidy's work, "The Fresh-water Rhizopods of North America," by the United States Government, this was equally true of the fresh-water Rhizopods, but now that difficulty has been entirely removed, and the student will find all the necessary information about the habits and forms of these organisms in that single volume. As an introduction to the study, this work will, it is hoped, be highly valued by those who cannot obtain the larger one, which, being a Government publication, will necessarily be limited in its distribution.

There is a broad field for valuable, original investigation in the study of the Rhizopods. We know comparatively little about their modes of reproduction and propagation—so little, indeed, that any observations whatever upon this subject will be of value, if carefully made.

The classification adopted by Professor Leidy has been followed in this book, and in the descriptions of genera and species the variations from the original have been very slight, and only such as have seemed advisable to make up for the lack of illustrative plates, or, in some cases, for the sake of brevity. It is believed that the descriptions will, in most cases, enable the student to name the specimens that he finds without the aid of figures.

Those who possess copies of Professor Leidy's work, and who have not made Rhizopods a special study, will find this book a valuable adjunct—a sort of key to the larger one; for the schematic synopses of genera and species will serve to lead the observer directly to the proper genus or species with a fair degree of certainty, by a hasty observation of the more prominent characteristics of the forms that may be discovered.

The careful study of Professor Leidy's work, which the preparation of this Synopsis has necessitated, has served to increase our admiration for his ability as an observer, and our appreciation of the great labor he has so conscientiously performed. Apart from the pleasure which an enthusiast always feels when engaged in his favorite study, Professor Leidy must find his reward mainly in his own knowledge of the lasting value of his book, and in the satisfaction of having done his work so well.

GENERAL CHARACTERISTICS OF RHIZOPODS.

Rhizopods consist, essentially, of a soft mass of clear or granular protoplasm, usually colorless, with one or more nuclei and contractile vesicles. By far, the greater number are provided with a shell-covering, sometimes chitinous but frequently composed of grains of sand and other extraneous matters cemented together.

A distinction is made between the outer protoplasmic layer and the interior mass of the body; the outer layer is called the ectosarc, the inner the endosarc. The distinction between endosarc and ectosarc is not always clear. There is no definite line of demarkation between them, such as would make the former correspond to a cell-wall. Dr. Wallich regards them as only temporarily distinct portions of sarcode, mutually convertible into one another. The ectosarc is merely a more or less thick layer of protoplasm, which seems to have undergone some change by contact with the surrounding medium. The endosarc is the interior protoplasmic mass; it is usually more coarsely granular than the ectosarc. Within the endosarc, the nuclei and the pulsating vesicles are found. The former are usually large, spherical, hyaline corpuscles, in most cases situated back of the middle of the animal. The pulsating or contractile vesicle is a colorless, or roseate, spherical structure, which is quite

common in Rhizopods, as well as in many forms of
Infusoria. Its true nature is not fully understood. It is
usually situated near the border of the endosarc, often
opening in the ectosarc, as in some of the Heliozoa—
the common *Actinophrys*, for example. The pulsating vesicles slowly enlarge until they attain a certain
size, after which they suddenly collapse and entirely
disappear; and this operation is repeated with a degree
of regularity.

The food of Rhizopods usually consists of diatoms,
desmids, and other algæ, and fragments of higher plants.
Within the body the food is usually accumulated in
spherical masses, which may be green, brownish or red ;
depending upon its nature and the changes which it
undergoes during digestion. Ehrenberg supposed that
the sperical masses indicated so many stomachs, and
therefore regarded the Rhizopods as belonging to his
Polygastrica. It is probable that the food is simply
enveloped by the protoplasm and becomes digested, after
which the hard portions may be thrown out at any part
of the surface of the body.

The most commonly observed process of multiplica-
tion is by division; in some species the body becomes
encysted, but the entire process has not yet been fully
made out.

Rhizopods are far more common in the ordinary collections of the microscopist than is generally supposed,

but since they are seldom looked for, they are often passed by unnoticed. For their study, however, systematic collections should be made, and for this purpose the superficial ooze at the bottom of still-water should be examined, after it has been allowed to settle for some time in a suitable dish. They are common in the slime of submerged rocks, stems and leaves, and especially so in moist sphagnum, and are to be found almost everywhere in moist situations not too much shaded, among decaying logs, mosses, lichens, and on the bark of trees.

In Professor Leidy's book, references to the literature of every species are given, with the names under which they have been described. In this book these names have been given as synonymes, with the names of the authors who have described them without the references. Those who possess the older works on the Infusoria, will doubtless find these synonymes of some assistance. The habitats given in the texts, are only intended to indicate where the species are likely to be found; and too much importance should not be attached to them in naming specimens.

The index is arranged to serve as a check-list, so that the student can readily keep a record of the species that he may find.

Measurements are all given in micro-millimetres; or, as more conveniently named, in micras. A micra is the one one-thousandth part of a millimetre (0.001^{mm}), and is designated by the Greek letter μ; it is equal to the 0.00039 ($\frac{1}{2540}$) of an inch. Ten micras are marked 10$^\mu$, four and a-half micras, 4.5$^\mu$.

According to the old system, 10μ would be called "one one-hundredth of a millimetre," 4.5μ would be forty-five ten-thousandths of a millimetre. It is, therefore, much simpler to apply the term micra in all microscopical measurements.

CLASS RHIZOPODA.

Order I.—PROTOPLASTA.

Nearly all the fresh-water Rhizopods belong to this order. They are either naked or covered with a chitinoid or siliceous shell, and move by the aid of pseudopodal projections of the sarcode body.

Order II.—HELIOZOA.

Body spherical, with many vacuoles or clear globules which give it a foamy appearance; usually a single nucleus, but sometimes several, and distinct contractile vesicles. Pseudopodia delicate, granular, emanating from all parts of the body, commonly simple and tapering, rarely forked or anastomosing, usually straight but highly flexible and contractile.

Order III.—RADIOLARIA.

Marine. Skeleton siliceous.

Order IV.—FORAMINIFERA.

Mostly marine. Shell usually calcareous.

Order V.—MONERA.

Without organs, body free and naked, composed of structureless sarcode.

Order I.—Protoplasta.

The Protoplasta include nearly all fresh-water forms except the Heliozoa. Naked or provided with an exterior chitinoid, or siliceous shell. There are two sub-orders.

Sub-Order I.—Lobosa.—Pseudopods are lobose projections from the clear ectosarc, simple, often more or less ramose, but never anastomosing, blunt or pointed.

Endosarc granular, not distinctly differentiated from the ectosarc, containing large, colorless or yellowish, sometimes bright green, spherical corpuscles, and one or more nuclei, and contractile vesicles. Reproduction by division.

Under certain conditions some of them become encysted, and the contents of the cysts may subdivide, or the nucleus may break up into what are apparently spermatozoids, and the endosarc into nucleated cells like ova.

The distinguishing characteristic of the Lobosa is the coarse, digitate form of the pseudopodia. In the Filosa the pseudopodia are usually much finer, and in the order Heliozoa they are like long rays, radiating from the centre of the spherical body of the animal.

Sub-Order II. — ***Filosa.*** — Pseudopods delicate and thread-like, having the same general constitution and form as in the shell-covered Lobosa, but never coarse or lobose, acutely forking, and becoming finer as they branch, rarely anastomosing.

Endosarc and ectosarc not distinctly differentiated, but the entire sarcode is homogeneous and resembles the endosarc of the Lobosa. Large, central, clear nucleus ; several peripheral contractile vesicles just below the nucleus. Reproductive process not fully made out.

SUB-ORDER I.—PROTOPLASTA LOBOSA.

Synopsis of the Genera of Lobosa.

		PAGE.
Form protean, ectosarc hyaline, endosarc granulous,	*Amœba,*	4
Similar to *Amœba*, but with trailing, filamentous appendages,	*Ouramœba,*	6
Similar to *Amœba*, but leech-like in form, somewhat differentiated into anterior and posterior parts, sometimes villous behind,	*Pelomyxa,*	7
Similar to *Amœba*, but slug-like, posterior papillose, body bristling with cils,* often with spicules,	*Dinamœba,*	9
Discoidal, endosarc distinctly colored, ectosarc colorless,	*Hyalodiscus,*	10

Body without a shell.

* Cils, a word used by Professor Leidy instead of *cilia*, meaning minute linear appendages, resembling fine hairs.

Body with a shell.

DESCRIPTION OF GENERA AND SPECIES.

Genus I.—Amœba.

When at rest, a spherical or oval mass of soft, hyaline, colorless, granular protoplasm. When in motion, form variable. Ectosarc hyaline and minutely granular. Endosarc continuous with the former, finely and coarsely granular, with corpuscles of varied character, ingesta of food, etc. Nuclei and one or more pulsating vacuoles. Pseudopodia digitate, simple or branched.

Amœba proteus.—In globular form, diameter 200μ in ovoidal form, 300μ by 150μ, extended in a dendroid form, 500μ in length by 400μ in breadth. This is one of the largest species. It is nearly colorless or more or less black by transmitted light, pale yellowish by reflected light. Pseudopodia digitate and blunt, sometimes tapering and pointed. Nucleus usually single, discoidal, posterior; contractile vesicle usually large and single, generally behind the nucleus. The special characteristic of this species is the digitate and blunt pseudopods.

A. verrucosa.—Mature animal, rather sluggish, irregularly oval, round or quadrately rounded form, with wartlike expansions, and a more or less wrinkled surface, as though invested with a membrane. Pseudopodia short, broad and blunt. Endosarc pale, granular, with few or no coarse granules. Ectosarc copious and hyaline. Contractile vesicle large. Nucleus usually distinct. Size ranging from 80μ by $\cdot72\mu$ to 180μ by 160μ. Very common.

Young animal actively moving, body oval or pyriform, usually moving with the broader pole in advance; surface comparatively smooth, but generally marked with four longitudinal lines or folds (*Amœba quadrilineata,* Carter); contractile vesicle posterior. Nucleus in front of the vesicle. Size from 40μ by 20μ to 120μ by 90μ.

A. radiosa.—SYN. : *A. radiosa,* Ehr., *brachiola,* Duj., *ramosa,* Duj.

Comparatively small, colorless and inactive. When floating free in the water stellate, with a spheroidal or oval central mass with from two to three, or a dozen or more, radiating pseudopods of variable length and form, mostly conical and acute or attenuated and thread-like, simple, straight, apparently rigid, curved or flexuose. On careful watching, the form may be observed to change very slowly, and the pseudopods to contract or elongate, or to bend or twist.

When creeping, of a less radiate character, but with pseudopods diverging mostly from one extremity in the direction of the movement. Contractile vesicle single, or several smaller ones. Nucleus usually distinct. Size, 12μ to 45μ, rarely 60μ in diameter; pseudopods 80μ long.

A. villosa.—SYN.: *Amœba*, Wallich; *A. villosa*, Wallich; *A. princeps*, Carter; *Trichamœba hirta*, Fromentel.

Animal in motion differentiated into an anterior and posterior region, sausage-shaped, irregularly clavate or palmate, and commonly with few lobate, or short, thick, digitate or conical pseudopods, mostly directed forward; posterior extremity commonly narrower, terminating in a villous process of variable form, usually rounded, knob-like or discoid. Endosarc, contractile vesicle and nucleus as in *A. proteus*. Size as large as 503μ.

No positively characteristic forms of this species have been observed in this country. The villous portions resemble protrusions of the endosarc.

GENUS II.—OURAMŒBA.

Animal possessing the same essential characteristics as the genus *Amœba*, but provided with fixed filamentous appendages habitually trailing from the posterior extremity of the body. Filaments flexible, cylindrical, tubular, inarticulate or articulate, resembling mycelial threads of fungi, perfectly passive.

Ouramœba vorax.—Syn. : *A. villosa,* Wallich; *O. vorax,* Leidy; *O. lapsa,* Leidy.

Animal in all respects resembling *A. proteus* with the addition of fascicles of trailing filaments. Filaments cylindrical tubes, each fascicle emanating from a common stalk, inarticulate, usually blunt at the ends; fascicles one to half a dozen or more, mostly trailing in a single bunch. Size: small form 140μ long by 280μ wide; filaments, 40μ to 180μ long. Rare.

O. botulicauda, Leidy.—Species comparatively small, colorless, transparent, angular. Pseudopods short, conical, acute, rarely digitate. Caudal appendages in one or two tufts, each composed of two to nine acutely divergent, segmented filaments of variable length. One or two contractile vesicles and nucleus present. This may be a young form of the preceding genus. The trailing filaments are usually in a single tuft, but occasionally there are two. Size : ranging from 40μ by 32μ to 76μ by 20μ; caudal appendages, 12μ to 45μ.

Genus III.—Pelomyxa.

Syn. : *Pelobius,* Greef ; *Pelomyxa,* Greef.

Animal like *Amœba,* naked, form variable ; when quiescent, spheroidal or ovoidal ; in motion, more or less leech-like or slug-like in shape ; differentiated into an anterior and a posterior region, habitually with the broader extremity in advance and progressing by the projection of a wave-like expansion of clear ectosarc in front or from other parts of the body ; frequently terminating posteriorly in a conspicuous process of clear sarcode

which is prehensile and often finely villous. Ectosarc clear; endosarc finely granular, containing vacuoles
and colorless globules. Nuclei numerous, scattered.
Contractile vesicles small and inconspicuous, except in
young forms. Voracious, usually gorged with vegetal
matter, with mud and sand.

Pelomyxa villosa.—Syn.: *A. sabulosa*, Leidy.

Almost opaque, except when young. By transmitted
light, brown or black, with hyaline border, yellowish-
white or cream-colored, and maculated with other colors,
according to the food; spheroidal or ovoidal in the resting
condition; clavate or botuliform when in motion, with
a terminal, sucker-like, villous patch; villi numerous, minute, papillary or filiform, simple or ramose. Pseudopods
usually one or two broad, lobal, anterior projections, rarely
prolonged or branching, sometimes accompanied by a
few narrow, conical processes of clear ectosarc from any
part of the body. Nuclei numerous, scattered. Contractile vesicles numerous, small. This species closely resembles *A. villosa*, and it is difficult sometimes to determine to
which of the two species a given form belongs. However,
the *A. villosa* is usually more distinctly elongated or
clavate in shape, and the pseudopods are rather more
slender than in *Pelomyxa*, while the villous process
is always present. In the latter the villi may be very
inconspicuous or even quite drawn in, and it is provided
with several small nuclei, not with a single large one
like *A. villosa*. Sand-grains are not conspicuous in
A. villosa. Size, while at rest, from 120μ to 1,250μ, but
commonly from 250μ to 500μ; when elongated, from
120μ by 60μ to 600 by 220μ, or larger.

Genus IV.—Dinamœba.

Animal of essentially the same structure as *Amœba*, spheroidal or oval when at rest, ovoid or slug-like when in motion, with the broader extremity in advance. Pseudopods few or many, mostly simple, subulate or long, conical and acute, occasionally furcate. Posterior extremity of the body papillose; papillæ variable, few or many, simple or compound, retractile. Surface of the body, pseudopods and papillæ bristling with minute spicules or motionless cils. Body often enveloped with a thick layer of hyaline jelly, with minute, imbedded spicules. Spicules of the body and of the jelly sometimes absent.

Dinamœba mirabilis. — SYN. : *Deinamœba mirabilis*, Leidy ; *A. tentaculata*, Leidy ; *Dinamœba*, Leidy.

Body round, oval, ovate or slug-like, more or less depressed, anteriorly broad and blunt, posterior part more narrow and more or less tapering ; spheroidal while floating. Pseudopods usually numerous, and usually anterior, moderately long, conical or fusiform. Posterior extremity of the body papillose. Surface of body, pseudopods and papillæ, thickly bristling with cils, which may be absent in some conditions. Nucleus and contractile vesicle usually obscured by other constituents. The large proportion of ectosarc reminds one of *A. verrucosa*. In size, form, and some other respects, it resembles *Pelomyxa villosa*, but in *Dinamœba* the pseudopods are numerous while they are not so in *Pelomyxa*. Like the latter it is very voracious. Its favorite food seems to be desmids, and it commonly occurs with *Didimoprium* and *Bam-*

busina. Size : in the spheroidal form, 64μ to 160μ; creeping forms, 152μ by 60μ to 340μ by 220μ.

Genus V.—Hyalodiscus.

Syn. : *Hyalodiscus*, H. and L. ; *Plakopus*, Schulze.

Body naked, discoidal, consisting of a colored, granular endosarc, with nucleus and vacuoles, and a clear, colorless ectosarc, which in the motion of the animal extends in a broad zone beyond the colored mass of endosarc, and projects pointed, conical processes, mostly few in number.

H. rubicundus.—Syn. : *H. rubicundus*, H. and L.; *Plakopus ruber* (?) Schulze.

Endosarc brick-red, composed of fine, red granules with a few larger ones of a darker shade, or else of conspicuous, globular, colored corpuscules mingled with fine granules. Size : 30μ to 60μ. [If *Plakopus ruber* is identical with this, it is much larger, being 200μ to 600μ.]

Genus VI.—Difflugia.

Syn. : *Difflugia*, Leclerc ; *Arcella*, Ehr.; *Lecquereusia*, Schlum.; *Homœochlamys, Heterocosmia, Exassula*, Ehr.

Shell variable in shape, usually composed of angular particles of quartz-sand, mingled with diatom frustules, spicules, etc., sometimes of chitinoid membrane, incorporated with extraneous particles, or composed in part or entirely of particles of a peculiar character. Mouth inferior, terminal, rarely sub-terminal. Sarcode almost filling the shell, attached by threads of ectosarc to the interior of the fundus and sides, and by a prolongation to the margin of the mouth. Nucleus single, near the fundus of the ectosarc. Contractile vesicles several, contiguous to the nucleus. Pseudopods, as many as six or more, cylindrical, simple or branching, commonly rounded at the ends, sometimes spreading and pointed.

Synopsis of Species of Difflugia.

Difflugia globulosa.—Syn.: *D. globulosa,* Duj.; *D. proteiformis,* Ehr. and Wallich; *D. globularis,* Wallich; *D. acropodia,* H. and L.

Shell spheroidal or oval, mouth inferior, terminal, circular, usually truncating the shell; sometimes protruding, rarely inverted. Shell composed of quartz-sand, diatoms, or of chitinoid membrane with sand and diatoms. Sarcode, apart from food, colorless. Size : smallest, with shell of sand, 36μ long by 30μ broad, mouth 15μ wide; chitinoid specimens, 24μ to 108μ long by 32μ to 120μ broad.

Hab.—In the ooze of ditches and ponds, or on moist earth in bogs, among mosses, etc.

Difflugia pyriformis.—SYN.: *Difflugia*, Leclerc, Carter ; *D. pyriformis*, Perty, Ehr., *proteiformis*, Lamarck, Ehr., Wallich, *compressa*, Carter, *entochloris*, Leidy, *vas*, Leidy, *nodosa*, Leidy, *cornuta*, Leidy.

Shell pyriform, flask-shaped or ovoid, with narrow pole prolonged into a neck of variable length, circular or somewhat compressed ; fundus obtusely rounded or subacute or produced into one to three conical processes. Neck gradually and evenly narrowed to the oral end, cylindroid, sometimes constricted, mouth inferior, terminal, circular or oval. Shell usually composed of angular particles of quartz-sand mingled with diatoms. Sarcode bright green, from chlorophyll grains. Common. The form of the shell varies greatly from pear-shaped to flask-like, the body gradually prolonged into a cylindroid or tapering neck. Size : 60μ to 580μ long by 40μ to 240μ wide; mouth 16μ to 120μ wide.

Hab.—Ooze of ponds, ditches and bogs.

Variety I.—*D. pyriformis.*

Variety II.—*D. compressa*, laterally compressed.

Variety III.—*D. nodosa*, fundus with eminences.

Variety IV.—*D. cornuta*, fundus with conical processes.

Variety V.—*D. vas*, neck defined by a constriction.

Difflugia urceolata.—Syn. : *D. urceo.ata,* Carter, *lageniformis,* Wallich, *proteiformis,* Wallich, *amphora,* Leidy, *olla,* Leidy.

Shell amphora-form, body spheroidal, ovate or ovoid, fundus obtusely and evenly rounded, more or less acute or acuminate, rarely bearing blunt spines (*D. olla*). Neck short, contracted, mouth large, circular, terminal, with or without a rim, usually reflected or everted. Shell commonly of hyaline quartz-sand. Sarcode, colorless ; pseudopods many, digitate, simple and branching. Size : spheroidal forms, 180μ to 440μ long by 140μ to 380μ broad ; ovoid forms, 200μ to 520μ long by 140μ to 360μ broad.

Hab.—Ditches and ponds, sphagnous swamps.

Difflugia cratera.—Syn. : *D. cratera,* Leidy.

Shell goblet-shaped, with oval or spheroidal body and wide, cylindroid neck ; fundus obtuse; mouth terminal, large, circular, truncating the neck, or with a reflected rim ; composed of colorless, chitinoid membrane, with particles of sand and dirt. [It is possible that these shells pertain to the ciliated infusorian of the genus *Tintinnus.*] Size : 56μ to 66μ long by 36μ to 42μ wide ; breadth of neck, 28μ to 36μ.

Hab.—Among Ceratophyllum and aquatic plants.

Difflugia acuminata.—Syn. : *Difflugia,* Leclerc ; *D. acuminata,* Ehr., Perty, *bacillariarum,* Perty, *pyriformis,* Carter, *proteiformis,* Wallich ; *D. Corticella acuminata,* Ehr.

Shell amphora-form or oblong, oval pyriform or cylindroid, with the upper part inflated ; fundus acute, acuminate or prolonged into a nipple-shaped process, rarely

with two or three points; neck long, short or none;
mouth large, terminal, circular; lip usually straight;
composed of angular quartz-sand, sometimes of diatom
remains, sometimes of chitinoid membrane. Sarcode
colorless. Common. Size: smallest specimens with shell
of sand, 100μ long by 48μ broad; large, pyriform specimens, 400μ long by 184μ broad; largest, 520μ by
120μ.

Hab.—Ponds and ditches.

Difflugia lobostoma.—SYN.: *D. proteiformis*, Carter, *tricus-*
pis, Carter, *oblonga*, Fresenius, *exassula tricuspis*, Ehr., *lobostoma*, Leidy,
crenulata, Leidy.

Shell ovoid, oval, or nearly spherical, usually composed
of quartz-sand, rarely with diatoms, or of chitinoid membrane with a few quartz particles; mouth terminal,
usually three to six lobed, or more; fundus obtusely
rounded. Sarcode colorless, or with green endosarc;
pseudopods up to six or more. One of the most common species. The conjugation of two and sometimes of
three individuals has been observed. Size: ordinarily
120μ long and 100μ broad. [The shell is usually ovoid,
and closely resembles *D. globulosa*, for which it may
readily be mistaken unless a view of the mouth, which
is commonly tri-lobed, can be obtained.]

Difflugia arcula.

Shell hemispheroidal; fundus convex; base inverted,
shallow infundibuliform; mouth inferior, central, tri-
lobed. Shell usually of yellowish, chitinoid membrane,
mostly with more or less adherent dirt, or scattered particles of quartz-sand or diatoms, especially occupying the

fundus. Common, perhaps an extreme variety of *lobostoma*. Size: 112μ to 144μ broad, by 60μ to 80μ high; mouth 28μ to 40μ. [This form differs from the preceding species principally by the yellowish color of the . shell.]

Hab.—Sphagnous swamps.

Difflugia corona.—Syn. : *D. corona, proteiformis*, Wallich.

Shell spherical or spheroidal, composed of clear, angular quartz-sand ; fundus with conical spines ; mouth terminal, circular, with multidentate or crenulate border. Sarcode colorless or brownish ; pseudopods many. A common form, but one of the most beautiful of the genus. The denticles are thick, angular processes, usually twelve in number, ranging from six to sixteen. The spines range from one to eleven, usually three to seven, arranged in an eccentric circle, divergent, equidistant, often a central spine is larger than the others. Size from 140μ to 320μ in diameter ; mouth 60μ to 180μ wide ; spines 40μ to 60μ long.

Hab.—Marshes, ponds, etc.

Difflugia constricta.—Syn. : *Arcella constricta, lunata, Arctiscon, guatimalensis*, Ehr. ; *D. marsupiformis, proteiformis*, Wallich ; *A. Homœochlamis constricta* and *lunata*, Ehr. ; *A. Heterocosmia Arctiscon* and *guatimalensis*, Ehr. ; *A. borealis, laticeps*, Ehr.

Shell laterally ovoid, fundus more or less prolonged obliquely upward, obtusely rounded and simple, or provided with spines. Mouth antero-inferior, large, circular or oval and inverted, with the anterior lip often prominent. Shell as usually seen by transmitted light, lying on the front, more or less pyriform, with the narrower part downward, and including the mouth, which appears as a clearer transversely oval, reniform or circular space; composed of quartz-sand or chitinoid membrane, colorless, yellowish or brown. Sarcode colorless.

A very common species. When erect, the axis, passing from the centre of the mouth to the summit of the shell is oblique, not perpendicular as in the preceding species. The bottom of the shell is concave, and the mouth is inflected and situated above the plane of the border of the base. Size: spineless forms, from 90μ long by 78μ broad to 232μ long by 160μ broad; spine-bearing forms from 180μ long by 120μ broad, to 340μ long to 180μ broad.

Hab.—Ooze of ponds.

Difflugia spiralis.—Syn.: *Difflugia*, Leclerc; *D. spiralis*, Ehr., Bail., Fres., Pritchard, Carter, Wallich, Leidy; *Lecquereusia jurassica*, Schlumberger; *D. proteiformis*, Wallich.

Shell retort-shaped, body usually spheroidal, laterally compressed, with a short, wide, cylindrical neck, obtuse fundus and circular or oval terminal mouth. Within the shell is a partition defining the neck from the body and giving to the shell, by transmitted light, the appearance of a single turn of a spiral. Size: length 96μ to 188μ; breadth, 68μ to 164μ; thickness, 68μ to 136μ.

Hab.—Sphagnous and cedar swamps.

Genus VII.—Hyalosphenia.

Syn.: *Hyalosphenia*, Stein; *Difflugia*, Tatem; *Catharia*, Leidy.

Shell compressed, ovoid to pyriform, composed of transparent, chitinoid membrane; mouth terminal, inferior, transversely elliptical. Sarcode occupying the interior of the shell to a variable extent, attached to the inner surface by threads and also to the border of the mouth. Nucleus large and central; contractile vesicles several; pseudopods digitate, few.

Synopsis of the Genera of Hyalosphenia.

	PAGE.
Shell compressed ovoid, very delicate, colorless; sarcode colorless,	*Cuneata*, 17
Shell compressed ovoid, in narrow view oral end notched; sarcode green,	*Papilio*, 18
Shell compressed pyriform, pale yellow, with pair of pores on border, short neck; sarcode colorless,	*Tincta*, 18
Shell compressed flask-shaped, long cylindroid neck; oral end in narrow view deeply notched, color brownish, longitudinal rows of pits,	*Elegans*, 19

Hyalosphenia cuneata.—SYN.: *H. cuneata*, Stein; *Difflugia ligata*, Tatem; *Catharia ligata*, Leidy; *Hyalosphenia lata*, Schulze; *H. ligata*, Leidy.

Shell compressed ovoid, in narrow view conical and truncate at the oral end, laterally and at the fundus convex; mouth terminal, oval; in broader view fundus convex with tapering borders, plane, convex or concave in their descent to the mouth. Shell composed of delicate, colorless membrane. Sarcode colorless, pyriform; pseudopods digitate, usually only one or two. The shell is so delicate that the tension of the threads of ectosarc is sufficient to bend it. Rare. Size: length 60μ to 76μ; breadth, 44μ to 60μ; thickness, 20μ; mouth 16μ by 12μ.

Hab.—In ponds.

Hyalosphenia papilio.—Syn. : *Difflugia (catharia) papilio,* Leidy ; *H. papilio,* Leidy.

Shell compressed oblong, ovoid, or compressed pyriform ; in the broader view the fundus transversely convex, and sides gradually tapering to the slightly convex oral end, or with a pyriform outline ; in the narrower view the fundus angularly rounded and the oral end notched. Mouth transversely oval, with rounded commissures. Shell yellowish, transparent ; endosarc bright green from chlorophyll ; pseudopods colorless, digitate, up to six in number. Size : length, 108μ to 140μ; breadth, 68μ to 84μ ; thickness, 32μ to 40μ by 8μ.

Hab.—In moist sphagnum ; not found in ponds.

Hyalosphenia tincta.

Shell compressed pyriform, relation of length to breadth variable, in transverse section compressed oval, of pale yellow, transparent, chitinoid membrane ; mouth transversely oval. Sarcode colorless ; pseudopods digitate, two, three or more. Like *H. cuneata* but more pyriform, shell colored, and lives in sphagnum instead of in ponds. Neck very short. Shell is thicker and less flexible than that of *H. cuneata,* and a pair of pores is to be seen on the lateral borders, usually below the middle, sometimes another pair above. It is probable that *H. tincta* merges into *H. cuneata,* and likewise into *H. elegans* and *H. papilio.* Size : length, 76μ to 92μ; breadth, 56μ to 64μ ; mouth, 20μ by 8μ.

Hab.—Sphagnous swamps and moist sphagnum.

Hyalosphenia elegans.—Syn.: *Difflugia (catharia) elegans,* Leidy.

Shell compressed flask-shaped ; in broad side view, oval body and long cylindroid neck, slightly widened at oral end,which is convex downward ; narrow side long elliptical, tapering to the oral end, which is deeply notched. Shell of pale brownish, transparent, structureless, chitinoid membrane, impressed with longitudinal rows of hemispherical pits. Sarcode colorless, attached by threads to the fundus of the shell; pseudopods digitate, usually three or four. This may be the same as Ehrenberg's *Difflugia spirigera.* Common. Size: length, 88µ to 108µ; breadth, 64µ to 40µ; thickness, 20µ to 28µ.

Hab.—Associated with *H. papilio* in sphagnum.

Genus VIII.—Quadrula.

Syn. : *Difflugia,* Wallich ; *Assulina, Hologlypha,* Ehr.; *Quadrula,* Schulze.

Shell compressed pyriform, transparent, composed of thin, square plates of chitinoid membrane, arranged in transverse or more or less oblique series in consecutive or alternating order. Mouth inferior, terminal, oval. Sarcode colorless.

Quadrula symmetrica.—Syn.: *Difflugia proteiformis, pyriformis, symmetrica,* Wallich ; *D. Assulina assulata, D. Carolinensis, leptolepis,* Ehr. ; *Quadrula symmetrica,* Schulze.

Shell compressed pyriform ; viewed on broad side with fundus widely convex, and sides sloping or more or less inflected toward the oral end, which is convex downward ; narrower side ellipsoidal, fundus obtuse, oval end roundly notched. Shell colorless, composed of square plates, arranged in transverse longitudinal or oblique rows. Sarcode colorless; pseudopods digitate, one to three or more. Size: length, 80μ to 140μ; breadth, 40μ to 960μ; thickness, 28μ to 48μ.

Hab.—Dripping rocks, ditches, sphagnum.

Genus IX.—Nebela.

Syn. : *Difflugia, Reticella, Allodictya, Odontodictya,* Ehr.; *Nebela,* Leidy.

Shell usually compressed pyriform, transparent, colorless, with or without appendages, composed of cancellated membrane, or of peculiar intrinsic elements of variable form and size, mostly of circular or oval discs, or narrow rectangular plates or rods, or of thin, less regular, angular plates, sometimes of chitinoid membrane incorporated with extrinsic elements, and sometimes of the latter entirely, as in *Difflugia.* Mouth inferior, terminal, oval. Sarcode colorless, same as in *Difflugia, Hyalosphenia,* etc.

Synopsis of the Species of Nebela.

Nebela collaris.—Syn. : *Difflugia collaris, reticulata, cancellata, carpio, binodis, annulata, laxa,* D. *Reticella collaris,* D. R. *reticullata,* D. R. *cancellata,* D. R. *carpio,* D. R. *binodis,* D. R. *annulata,* D. R. *laxa,* D. *cellulifera,* Ehr.; D. *peltigeracea,* Carter; D. *symmetrica,* Wallich ; D. (*Nebela*) *numata,* Leidy ; *Nebela numata,* Leidy.

Shell compressed pyriform, longer than broad ; viewed on broad side, fundus widely convex, sloping sides usually slightly inflected toward the oral end, which is convex downward ; in the narrow view oblong, fundus obtuse, sometimes impressed on each side, gradually sloping, and usually inflected toward the oral end, which is concavely notched. Mouth transversely oval, entire. Shell colorless, variable in its structural elements, generally composed of oval or circular disks, uniform or variable in size, sometimes mingled with rod-like plates, or almost wholly composed of them, rarely of thin, irregular, angular plates. In some specimens the transversal section is hexahedral, with concave sides and prominent, rounded angles. Sarcode colorless, pseudopods digitate usually 3–6. Common. [A single specimen was observed by Prof. Leidy, with a curved or retort-shaped shell, 150μ long by 72μ, and 36μ in section.] Size : usually 100μ to 140μ in length ; average 128μ long, 80μ broad, and 48μ thick ; mouth 32μ by 24μ.

Hab.—Moist sphagnum ; a constant associate of *Hyalosphenia papilio* and *elegans.*

Nebela flabellulum.—Syn. : *Difflugia* (*Nebela*) *flabellulum, N. flabellulum,* Leidy.

Shell compressed pyriform or spheroid, usually broader than long, sometimes not ; transverse section oval, with rounded angular poles ; neck short or none ; mouth transversely oval, slightly convex downward, in the long diameter. Shell, sarcode and pseudopods, like those of *N. collaris.* Common. Size: length, 68μ to 96μ; breadth, 72μ to 104μ; thickness, 32μ to 48μ; mouth, from 24μ by 12μ to 20μ by 12μ.

Hab.—Sphagnous swamps.

Nebela carinata.—SYN.: *Difflugia carinata,* Archer ; *N. carinata,* Leidy.

Shell resembling in shape and structure that of *N. collaris,* but provided with a thin keel of chitinoid membrane, beginning above the neck and extending along the lateral borders over the fundus. Sarcode like that of *N. collaris.* Size: length, 144μ to 240μ; breadth, 88μ to 168μ; thickness, 40μ to 72μ; mouth, 36μ by 20 to 28μ by 28μ; carina, from 4μ to 20μ deep.

Hab.—Sphagnous swamps.

Nebela hippocrepis.—SYN.: *Difflugia (Nebela) equicalceus, N. equicalceus,* Leidy.

Shell compressed pyriform, with thick, blunt, solid carina extending around the fundus and lateral borders, and ending in long, digitate processes projecting downward into the interior of the cavity. Mouth transversely oval, convex downward. Shell transparent, colorless, composed of circular disks; carina pale straw colored, indistinctly granular. Sarcode, as in *N. collaris* and *carinata.* Size: length, 252μ to 260μ; breadth, including carina, 140μ to 160μ; thickness, 68μ to 72μ; mouth, 40μ by 28μ; carina, 16μ and 8μ deep.

Hab.—Sphagnum.

Nebela ansata.—Syn. : *Difflugia (Nebela) ansata, N. ansata,* Leidy.

Shell compressed pyriform, with a pair of lateral, conical offsets or spurs diverging upward from the neck, but otherwise like *N. collaris.* Size: length, 216μ to 260μ; breadth, between ends of lateral horns, 132μ to 164μ, at the fundus, 104μ to 120μ; thickness, 60μ to 64μ; mouth, 40μ to 52μ by 28μ.

Hab.—Sphagnum of cedar swamp.

Nebela barbata.—Syn. : *Difflugia (Nebela) barbata, N. barbata,* Leidy.

Shell bottle-form, slightly compressed, with cylindroid neck about as long as the ovoidal body; fundus obtuse, oval end slightly expanded, convex downward in the longer diameter; transparent, colorless, composed of circular disks and provided with short, stiff cils, which apparently project from the spaces between the disks; mouth oval, entire. Size: length, 80μ to 120μ; breadth, 44μ to 56μ; thickness, 36μ to 48μ; mouth, 16μ to 24μ wide.

Hab.—Sphagnum of cedar swamp.

Nebela caudata.

Shell compressed ovoid, with four or five hollow, narrow, blunt, conical or clavate processes projecting from the lateral borders, and summit of the fundus. Mouth transversely oval, convex downward.

Shell transparent, colorless, in structure resembling *N. collaris*, but usually less distinct. Sarcode colorless. Rare. Length, exclusive of processes, 80μ; breadth, 60μ; thickness, 32μ; mouth, 20μ by 16μ; length of processes, 16μ to 24μ.

Genus X.—Heleopera.

Shell compressed ovoid, composed of cancellated, chitinoid membrane, presenting a reticulated appearance of mostly dotted or interrupted lines, often incorporated with particles of sand at the fundus. Mouth inferior, terminal, large, transversely elliptical. Sarcode as in *Hyalosphenia* and *Nebela*. Pseudopods numerous, digitiform.

Heleopera picta.—Syn.: *Difflugia (Nebela) sphagni, Nebela sphagni,* Leidy.

Shell compressed ovoid, never pyriform, with the oral pole narrower; mouth terminal, forming a long, narrow ellipse with acute commissures, convex downward, acutely notched on the narrow sides; composed of a yellowish, transparent, chitinoid membrane with a reticular structure, meshes polygonal and lines of the net dotted. Sarcode with bright-green endosarc, owing to numerous chlorophyll vesicles. Pseudopods digitate, simple and branched, large and numerous, often writhing, snake-like. Length, 92μ to 168μ; breadth, 76μ to 136μ; thickness, 44μ to 72μ; mouth, 36μ by 16μ to 72μ by 32μ.

Hab.—Sphagnous swamps.

Heleopera petricola.

Shell compressed oval; mouth terminal, broad, elliptical, convex downward, with acute commissures in the narrow view; fundus convex, loaded with quartz grains; composed of chitinoid membrane, reticular, with polygonal or rounded meshes, colorless or brownish. Length, 96μ to 150μ; breadth, 68μ to 90μ, and 48μ to 60μ; breadth of mouth, 52μ to 60μ by 15μ.

Hab.—Sphagnous swamps.

Genus XI.—Arcella.

Shell composed of chitinoid membrane, never of extrinsic elements, with a minutely hexagonal cancellated structure, translucent and commonly of a brown color, variable in shape, but usually more or less campanulate, with a circular base, concavely infundibuliform and convex at the border, and with the mouth central. Sarcode occupying the central portion of the shell, connected with the mouth by a cylindrical neck, and by means of threads of ectosarc with the dome of the shell. Pseudopods few, blunt, digitate, simple or branching. Commonly two nuclei, one on each side. Contractile vesicles several, occupying the periphery.

Synopsis of the Species of Arcella.

		PAGE.
Shell hemispherical or bell-shaped, height half the breadth, widest at the base,	*Vulgaris*,	25
Shell discoid or shield-shaped, height one-fourth or one-third the breath,	*Discoides*,	26
Shell mitriform or balloon-shaped, height exceeding the diameter of base; widest near the middle,	*Mitrata*,	26
Shell viewed from above circular and dentate, from the side crown-like; breadth more than twice the height,	*Dentata*,	27
Shell basal-border everted, rising to $\frac{1}{4}$ or $\frac{1}{2}$ the height of the shell, obtusely angular; from $\frac{1}{4}$ to $\frac{1}{2}$ as high as broad,	*Artocrea*,	27

Arcella vulgaris.—Syn.: *A. vulgaris, dentata, A. sticholepis vulgaris, A. Homœochlamis angulosa*, Ehr.; *A. hemispherica, angulosa, viridis*, Perty; *Arcellina vulgaris*, Carter.

Shell hemispherical or campanulate; height about half the breadth, widest across the usually slightly expanded and circular base, which is inferior, convex at the border, and concavely inverted infundibuliform centrally to the mouth. Dome evenly convex or angularly faceted or concavely pitted at the summit and sides; the facets or pits variable in number, bounded by prominent folds and ranged in two or three circles. Mouth circular, · mostly entire, border rarely slightly crenulated. Sarcode mass oblately spheroidal, colorless, except from food. Pseudopods digitate, color of test from colorless to brown and deep blue. The shell sometimes appears like a truncated pyramid, with angular outline, such forms may be regarded as a variety *angulosa.* Size: breadth, 48μ to 152μ; height, 36μ to 72μ; mouth, 12μ to 48μ. Very common.

Hab.—Ooze of stagnant water and on submerged aquatic plants.

Arcella discoides.—Syn. : *A. discoides, peristicta,* Ehr.; *A. Homœochlamis discoides,* Ehr.; *A. Heterocosmia peristicta,* Ehr.

Shell circular, shield-shaped, usually with the length from one-fourth to one-third of the breadth; dome low, evenly convex to the rounded, or slightly expanded and rounded, basal-border; base, mouth, and color of shell as in *A. vulgaris.* Breadth, 72μ to 264μ; height, 20μ to 80μ; width, 20μ to 80μ.

Hab.—Everywhere in association with *A. vulgaris.*

Arcella mitrata.

Shell mitriform or balloon-shaped, obpyriform or polyhedral, higher than the breadth of the base, widest at or near the middle, more or less contracted or sloping inwardly toward the base; dome mostly inflated; summit and sides evenly rounded or depressed into broad, angular facets, bounded by prominent folds; base rounded at the border, inverted concavely infundibuliform; mouth circular, crenulated, mostly everted into the inverted funnel. Sarcode-mass spheroidal, usually connected with the mouth by a cylindrical neck. Pseudopods up to six or more. Height, 80μ to 180μ; breadth at base, 72μ to 168μ; at dome, 84μ to 200μ; mouth, 20μ to 80μ. Frequent.

Hab.—Ponds.

Arcella dentata.—Syn.: *A. dentata, stellata*, Ehr.; *A. stellaris, Okeni,* Perty ; *A. Homœochlamis dentata, A. Heterocosmia stellata, A. sticholepis stellaris,* Ehr.

Shell, as seen from above or below, circular and more or less dentate, resembling a wheel with pointed cogs, in side view crown-like; breadth more than twice the height; dome convex and even, or depressed at the summit, and broadly fluted at the sides; base centrally inverted, concavely infundibuliform, at the periphery more or less everted, and divided into projections of variable length. Mouth circular, entire. Sarcode like *A. vulgaris.* Shell colorless or brown. Breadth, between the points of the base, 132μ to 184μ; height, 44μ to 48μ; mouth, 40μ to 44μ. Not common.

Hab.—Same as *A. vulgaris.*

Arcella artocrea.

Shell from one-fourth to less than half as high as broad; dome convex and even, or mammillated or pitted; basal-border everted and rising from one-fourth to nearly one-half of the height of the shell, obtusely angular and entire; central portion of the base inverted in the usual

manner; mouth circular, entire, surrounded with a row
of minute tubercles.   Sarcode colored from bright-green
chlorophyll corpuscles in the endosarc.   Pseudopods digitate. Breadth at lateral border, 144μ to 176μ; at base, 112μ
to 136μ; height, 40μ to 60μ; mouth, 20μ to 28μ.   Rare.
Hab.—Ponds.

Genus XII.—Centropyxis.

SYN.: *Arcella, Homœochlamys,* Ehr.; *Difflugia,* Perty; *Centropyxis,*
Stein; *Echinopyxis,* C. and L.

Shell discoid, circular, oval or ovoid, deepest or thick-
est and most obtuse posteriorly, with the base on a level
inferiorly and deeply inflected to the mouth, with the
dome highest posteriorly, gently curving or sloping forward, more abruptly convex backward; mouth and fundus eccentric in opposite directions, the former anterior
and inferior, the latter posterior and even, or furnished
with a variable number of conical spines.   Mouth circular or oval and entire, or with sinuous border, and extending into appendages within, toward the dome.
Shell usually brown, but sometimes colorless, composed
of chitinoid membrane, mostly incorporated with variable proportions of sand, often in such quantity as to
resemble *Difflugia,* never cancellated as in *Arcella.*
Sarcode colorless.   Pseudopods digitate.

Centropyxis aculeata.—SYN.: *Arcella aculeata, ecornis, Dia-
dema, A, centropyxis aculeata, A. Homœochlamys ecornis, A. centropyxis,
Diadema,* Ehr.; *Difflugia aculeata,* Perty; *Centropyxis aculeata,* Stein;
Echinopyxis aculeata, C. and L., Carter, Barnard; *Centropyxis, C. ecornis*
Leidy.

Form exceedingly variable; seen from above it usually
appears broadly ovoid in outline, with the mouth nearer

the narrower pole and a variable number of spines diverging from the opposite pole and sides ; in the lateral view it is cap-shaped like *Difflugia constricta,* but more depressed; base rests on a level at its anterior two-thirds, and is inverted as in *Arcella.* The spines range from one to nine, or they may be absent (var. *ecornis*). Length, 88μ to 26μ ; breadth, 72μ to 220μ ; height, 36μ to 80μ; mouth, 28μ to 100μ ; length of spines, 20μ to 60μ.

Hab.—Common with *Arcella vulgaris,* among floating confervæ, or adherent to aquatic plants.

GENUS XIII.—COCHLIOPODIUM.

Animal minute, provided with a flexible, chitinoid shell, thinning away to the broadly expansive mouth, and exhibiting a minutely cancellated structure. Sarcode intimately adherent to every part of the interior of the shell, pale, granular, mingled with variable proportions of highly refractive corpuscles, often crystals and other elements, together with a large central nucleus, and one or more contractile vesicles. Pseudopods delicate, hyaline, conical, pointed, sometimes forked.

Cochliopodium bilimbosum.—SYN. : *Amœba bilimbosum, actinphora,* Auerbach ; *Amœba zonalis,* Leidy ; *Cochliopodium pellucidum,* H. and L., Schulze.

Body when at rest spheroid or ovoid ; by transmitted light, viewed from above, appearing usually as a translucent, granular, protoplasmic mass, with coarser, darkly outlined granules, closely invested by a transparent, colorless, doubly contoured, more or less distinctly punctate or cancellated membrane like young colorless shells of *Arcella.* When moving, usually more or less completely surrounded by a delicate, transparent zone, finely and regularly punctate. In the lateral view usually more or less bell-shaped, with the fundus and sides defined by a doubly contoured dotted line, and at the mouth with a more translucent, wide, punctate band, defined by a scarcely perceptible dentated edge. The shell is so closely adherent and so flexible that it accommodates itself to the changing form of the sarcode. Pseudopods few, conical or awl-shaped, often irregular and sometimes furcate. In spheroidal condition diameter 24μ to 56μ.

Hab.—Springs, ponds, ditches, among algæ and in ooze.

Cochliopodium vestitum. — SYN. : *Amphizonella vestita,* Archer ; *C. pilosum,* H. and L.; *C. vestitum,* Archer.

Body as in the preceding species, but more or less covered with minute, rigid cils. Diameter, 40μ to 60μ.

SUB-ORDER II.—PROTOPLASTA FILOSA.

Synopsis of the Genera of Filosa.

DESCRIPTION OF GENERA AND SPECIES.

Genus I.—Pamphagus.

SYN. : *Arcella, Homœochlamys*, Ehr.; *Gromia*, Schlumberger; *Corycie*, Duj.; *Difflugia*, Schneider ; *Pamphagus*, Bailey, C. and L., *Plagiophrys*, *Lecytheum*, H. and L.

Animal colorless, transparent, invested with a hyaline, structureless membrane, which is flexible and elastic, and concurs strictly with any changes of form of the body, but ordinarily restricts such changes and is not voluntarily extensible ; sarcode completely filling it, and appearing to be structurally continuous with it. Nucleus large and clear. Contractile vesicles not distinctly determined. Mouth small, terminal. Pseudopods filamentous, long, exceedingly delicate, branching dichotomously, not anastomosing.

Pamphagus mutabilis.—Syn.: *Corycie,* Duj.; *P. mutabilis,* Bailey; *Corycia Dujardini,* Gagliardi; *Plagiophrys scutiformis,* H. and L.

Animal compressed ovoid, ovate or subpyriform; lateral borders extending to the fundus acute; fundus in the greater breadth obtusely rounded, more or less acute or even acuminate; mouth small, transversely oval, with a thickened border. Sarcode pale, granular, colorless or yellowish. Food usually one-celled algæ. Animal in movement upright, mouth downward, pseudopods divergent and spreading. Length 40μ to 100μ; greater breadth, 28μ to 68μ.

Hab. — Ooze of springs and ponds, and sphagnous ponds.

Pamphagus hyalinus.—Syn.: *Arcella hyalina, A. Homœochlamys hyalina,* Ehr.; *Gromia hyalina,* Schlum.; *Difflugia enchelys,* Schneider; *Lecytheum hyalinum,* H. and L., Archer.

Animal spheroidal and slightly produced at the lower pole into a short, broad neck, terminating in a circular mouth. Shell membranous, transparent, colorless, structureless and elastic. Pseudopods filamentous and furcate. From 32μ in diameter to 48μ in length, and 44μ in breadth.

Hab.—Superficial ooze of ponds, ditches and lakes.

Pamphagus curvus.

Animal retort-shaped or ovoid, with the prolonged narrower pole curved, and with the body in transverse section circular. Mouth inferior, terminal, circular. Shell colorless or pale yellowish, structureless. Nucleus and pseudopods as in *P. mutabilis.* From 44μ in length by 28μ, to 60μ by 36μ.

Pamphagus avidus.—Body oval or ovoid, in transverse section circular, wider at the oral pole; mouth small, circular, contractile. Length, 148μ to 220μ; breadth, 120μ.

Hab.—Cedar swamp.

GENUS II.—PSEUDODIFFLUGIA.

SYN.: *Pseudodifflugia*, Schlum.; *Pleurophrys*, C. and L.

Animal provided with a thin, chitinoid shell, usually incorporated with variable proportions of fine quartz sand or other extrinsic material. Mouth terminal, inferior. Sarcode usually colorless, with a large, clear nucleus, but obscured by the nature of the shell. Pseudopods numerous, exceedingly delicate, filamentous and forking at acute angles.

Pseudodifflugia gracilis. — SYN.: *P. gracilis*, Schlum.; *Pleurophrys sphærica*, C. and L., H. and L., Schulze; *Pleurophrys* (?) *amphitremoides*, Archer, Schulze; *Pleurophrys* (?) *fulva*, Archer; *Pleurophrys compressa, lageniformis*, Schulze; *Pleurophrys angulata*, Mereschkowsky.

Shell of variable form, usually spheroidal, ovoidal or oblong oval, and of uniform transverse diameters and straight, but rarely compressed and slightly curved. Mouth terminal, circular; structure obscurely granular, often with fine sand, and frequently almost entirely composed of coarser sand, colorless or brownish. Length, 40μ to 160μ; breadth, 20μ to 100μ.

Hab.—Ooze of ponds, ditches, &c.

Genus III.—Cyphoderia.

Syn.: *Difflugia, Assulina, Ampullaria, Hologlypha,* Ehr. ; *Cyphoderia,* Schlum. ; *Euglypha,* Perty ; *Lagynis,* Schulze.

Shell retort-shaped, mouth downward, long axis inclined ; chitinoid, transparent, colored or colorless, composed of minute, hexagonal elements of uniform size, arranged in alternating series in parallel, spiral rows. Mouth minutely beaded. Sarcode pale, granular, usually nearly filling the shell. Nucleus large, clear, usually homogeneous. Contractile vesicles present. Pseudopods numerous, forking, mostly radiating in a horizontal plane.

Cyphoderia ampulla. — Syn.: *Difflugia ampulla, lagena, Seelandica, adunca, alabamensis, uncinata, hologlypha, D. Assulina adunca, D. A. alabamensis, D. A. ampulla, D. A. margaritacea, D. A. uncinata,* Ehr. ; *Cyphoderia margaritacea,* Schlum., Stein, Fresenius, Carter, H. and L., Leidy, Schulze ; *Euglypha curvata,* Perty ; *Lagynis baltica,* Schulze ; *Euglypha margaritacea, Difflugia margaritacea, Euglypha baltica,* Wallich ; *Cyphoderia ampulla,* Leidy.

Shell retort-shaped, neck short, cylindrical, curving downward and truncated by a circular mouth ; body oblong oval, longitudinal axis inclined but nearly horizontal ; fundus obtusely rounded, sometimes flattened, frequently prolonged into a nipple at the summit ; color yellowish or colorless. Length, from 112μ to 176μ ; breadth, from 40μ to 80μ ; mouth, 16μ to 28μ.

Hab.—Ooze of ponds, lakes and ditches.

Genus IV.—Campascus.

Shell shaped like *Cyphoderia,* but fundus provided with a pair of divergent, chitinoid processes.

Campascus cornutus.

Shell retort-shaped, neck short and curved; obtuse fundus directed backward and upward, with a divergent conical prolongation on each side ; composed of translucent, yellowish, chitinoid membrane incorporated with scattered particles of sand ; mouth circular, bordered by a delicate, colorless, annular expansion. Pseudopods furcate and very delicate. Length, 112μ to 140μ; breadth, 180μ; mouth, 24μ to 28μ.

Hab.—Ooze of China Lake, Wyoming Territory, at an altitude of 10,000 feet.

GENUS V.—EUGLYPHA.

SYN. : *Euglypha,* Duj. ; *Difflugia ; Assulina ; Setigerella,* Ehr.

Shell hyaline, ovoid, of uniform diameter or compressed, composed of regular rows of oval or hexagonal chitinoid plates, arranged in longitudinal series, the plates alternating with one another in the different rows. Mouth terminal, circular or elliptical, the marginal plates forming a series of minutely serrulate, angular points. Shell usually provided with spines or hairs. Sarcode colorless, with a large nucleus and contractile vesicles. Pseudopods filamentous, exceedingly delicate, dichotomously branching, not anastomosing, with no evident circulation of granules, more or less horizontally divergent.

Euglypha alveolata——SYN. : *E. alveolata,* Duj., Ehr., Pritchard and others ; *E. tuberculata,* Duj., C. and L., Pritchard, Perty ; *Difflugia areolata, acanthophora, levigata, striolata,* Ehr.; *E. lævis, setigera,*

Perty ; *Difflugia floridæ, pilosa, moluccensis, amphora, rectangularis,
D. Roberti, Müller, D. seriata, striata, Assulina alveolata, amphora,* etc.,
*Setigerella acanthophora, setigera, Difflugia Shannoniana, Difflugia
subacuta,* Ehr.

Shell transparent, colorless, usually regularly ovoid,
often oblong ovoid, sometimes flask-shaped ; in transverse
section circular, rarely compressed ; fundus broad, obtusely
rounded, rarely sub-acute ; oral end narrowest, often more
or less tapering. Mouth circular, surrounded with 4 to
12 (?) angular, denticulate points. Plates of the shell
usually oval, ovate or cordate (?), arranged in alternating
longitudinal rows, overlapping at the contiguous borders
so as to produce hexagonal areas included in zones of
minute, elliptical areolæ. Fundus with 4 to 6 spines,
usually straight and equidistant, divergent or convergent,
sometimes irregular — in smaller, less well-developed
forms, spines are absent. Length, 30μ to 152μ; breadth
18μ to 88μ.

Hab.—Among algæ, mosses, etc., in bogs and in moist
situations, and in ooze of ponds.

Euglypha ciliata. — Syn.: *Difflugia ciliata, pilosa, strigosa,
D. Setigerella strigosa,* Ehr. ; *Euglypha compressa,* Carter, Leidy,
Schulze ; *E. strigosa,* Leidy.

Shell compressed ovoid, with the oral pole usually
more or less tapering and truncated by the transversely
oval mouth ; transverse section oval, with rounded, more
or less sub-acute poles. Fundus and lateral borders
mostly fringed with spines or bristles, variable in number
and robustness, sometimes absent, sometimes numerous.
Plates mostly elongated hexahedral, closely fitting at the
margins. Mouth bordered with from 6 to 14 or more (?)

blunt, angular, crenulated teeth, composed of the lowest plates of the shell, which are usually thicker than the others. Length, 56μ to 100μ; greater breadth, 24μ to 60μ; less-breadth, 16μ to 32μ.

Hab.—Common in wet sphagnum, of sphagnous swamps.

Euglypha cristata.

Shell tubular, flask-shaped, moderately inflated toward the fundus, and tapering gradually to the slightly contracted mouth; circular in transverse section, hyaline, colorless, composed of overlapping oval plates, appearing as hexahedral areas, sometimes resembling hexagonal plates joined at the edges. Mouth round, 4 to 6 angular serrulated teeth. Fundus with a tuft of curved, radiating spines. Length, 40μ to 72μ; breadth, 10μ to 20μ.

Hab.—Sphagnous swamps.

Euglypha mucronata.

Shell like *E. cristata*, but with a conical, acute dome, prolonged into a long, mucronate spine, sometimes two. Length, 108μ to 140μ; breadth, 32μ to 44μ; mucro, 20μ to 44μ long.

Hab.—Wet sphagnum.

Euglypha brachiata.

Shell like *E. cristata*, but with a tuft of spines to the fundus, and with 2 to 4 to 6 long spines springing from the neck and diverging or curving upward and outward. Length, 104μ to 128μ; breadth, 28μ to 40μ.

Hab.—Wet sphagnum and ooze.

GENUS VI.—PLACOCISTA.

SYN. : *Euglypha,* Carter.

Shell compressed oval, hyaline, colorless, with acute border and terminal, elliptical mouth, the border of the latter entire, with acute commissures; plates of the longitudinal alternating rows oval, overlapping, so as to produce hexahedral areas limited by zones of minute ellipses. Lateral borders and fundus furnished with acuminate spines, articulated with the shell. Sarcode as in *Euglypha.* This genus differ from *Euglypha* by its entire mouth without dentate scales, and by its articulated spines.

Placocista spinosa.—SYN. : *Euglypha spinosa,* Carter, Archer, Leidy.

Shell transparent, colorless, compressed oval, with acute, lateral borders, sometimes slightly tapering toward the oral pole; mouth large, transversely elliptical, with acute commissures and entire, edentulous border; composed of oval, imbricating plates, in alternating longitudinal series, the overlapping borders producing hexahedral areas limited by zones of minute ellipses; oral row of plates like the others, and not forming angular teeth as in *Euglypha.* The lateral, acute border of the shell fringed with movable subulate spines articulated with the shell by a minute knob, usually in pairs, sometimes single and rarely triple. Length, 100μ to 136μ; breadth, 80μ to 96μ, and 36μ to 60μ; mouth, 40μ to 60μ; spines, 16μ to 40μ long.

Hab.—Moist sphagnum of cedar swamps.

Genus VII.—Assulina.

Syn. : *Difflugia, Euglypha, Assulina,* Ehr.

Shell compressed spherical or oval; neck almost obsolete, terminating in a transversely elliptical mouth, with uneven or ragged edges, composed of minute, oval or hexagonal plates in alternating rows. Sarcode and pseudopods as in *Euglypha.*

Assulina seminulum.—Syn. : *Difflugia seminulum, Euglypha seminulum, Difflugia semen,* Ehr. ; *Euglypha brunnea,* Leidy ; *E. tincta,* Archer ; *E. seminulum,* Leidy.

Shell nearly as broad as long, compressed, spheroidal or oval; breadth nearly equal to the length; thickness half or less than half the breadth ; dome and lateral borders rounded or sub-acute. Mouth transversely oval, and abruptly truncating the pole of the shell, or the latter may be prolonged into a short neck. Shell chocolate brown, sometimes quite light, and in young individuals colorless, usually lighter in color at the mouth ; composed of minute, oval or hexagonal plates, arranged in alternating longitudinal or obliquely parallel, spiral rows ; oral plates, lighter in color than the others, end in irregular processes. Sarcode usually occupies but little more than half the capacity of the shell, arranged about the axis. Pseudopods few and extremely delicate. Length, 50μ to 83μ ; breadth, 40μ to 71μ, and 16μ to 33μ thick.
Hab.—Sphagnum, often very abundant.

Genus VIII.—Trinema.

Shell hyaline, pouch-like, with its long axis inclined or oblique, with the mouth sub-terminal. Dome obtusely rounded ; mouth inverted, circular, minutely beaded at the border. Structure of the shell in the smallest forms apparently homogeneous, but in the larger ones composed of circular plates arranged in alternating series, and often appearing with a beaded margin. Sarcode and pseudopods as in *Euglypha.* When moving, the body is inclined, mouth downward, fundus directed upward and backward.

Trinema enchelis.—SYN. : *Trinème, Trinema,* Duj. ; *Difflugia enchelis, Arcella hyalina, constricta, A. Nidus pendulus, A. disphæra, caudicicola, enchelys, megastoma, rostrata, reticulata, seriata, pyrum ; Homæochlamys constricta,* etc., *Sticholepus caudicicola,* etc., *Heterocosmia pyrum,* Ehr. ; *Trinema acinus,* Duj. ; *T. enchelis,* Leidy.

The only species. One of the commonest shell-bearing rhizopods. Length, 16μ to 100μ; breadth, 10μ to 60 ; mouth, 5μ to 24μ.

Hab.—Ooze of pools and in moist places.

GENUS IX.—SPHENODERIA.

Shell globular or oval, sometimes slightly compressed, hyaline, membranous, with a short, broad neck, and a wide, elliptical, subterminal, or oblique (?) mouth ; body with circular, oval or hexagonal plates or cancelli, arranged in alternating series. Sarcode and pseudopods as in *Euglypha.*

Sphenoderia lenta.—SYN. : *S. lenta,* Schlum., Ehr. ; *Euglypha globosa,* Carter, H. and L., Schulze, Leidy ; *Assulina lenta,* Ehr.

Shell delicate, membranous, colorless, transparent, globular, oval or oblong ; sometimes slightly compressed, with a short, broad, compressed neck, widening toward the narrow, elliptical mouth, which is oblique or subterminal (?). Border of mouth thin, delicate, entire. Body of shell composed of circular or oval plates, overlapping at their contiguous borders and arranged in alternating series, apparently not extending to the neck. Sarcode as in *Euglypha* and *Trinema*. *Sphenoderia* is closely related to *Trinema;* and a variety with a denticulated mouth is nearly related to *Assulina seminulum*. Globose forms: length, 32μ to 56μ; breadth, 28μ to 52μ or to 56μ in diameter; oval forms: from 28μ to 56μ long, and 20μ to 44μ broad.

Hab.—Common in moist sphagnum and in bogs.

Sphenoderia macrolepis.

Shell pyriform, compressed, with a broad neck gradually extending from the body, and terminating in an oblique, elliptical mouth, and with the broader surfaces composed mainly of a pair of hexahedral plates, from which the neck is extended below. Length, 20μ to 28μ.

Hab.—Sphagnous swamp.

Order II.—Heliozoa.

The *Heliozoa* or sun-animalcules are usually of a spherical form, with pseudopodal filaments radiating from them in every direction, rarely forking or anastomosing. They usually multiply by division. While the Lobosa and the Filosa are essentially creeping animals, the Heliozoa, or sun animalcules, are swimmers.

Synopsis of the Genera of Heliozoa.

DESCRIPTION OF GENERA AND SPECIES.

GENUS I.—ACTINOPHRYS.

Body soft, spherical, composed of hyaline, colorless, pale and finely granular protoplasm, with mingled coarser granules and minute oil-like molecules, more or less crowded with large, clear vesicles or vacuoles. Nucleus central, ordinarily obscured. A large contractile vesicle at the periphery. Pseudopods numerous, projecting as exceedingly delicate, tapering rays, or finely granular extensions of the protoplasm of the surface; not branching.

Actinophrys sol.—SYN.: *Trichoda sol*, Müller, Schrank; *Peritricha sol*, Bory; *Actinophrys sol*, Ehr., Pritchard and others; *A. difformis*, Ehr.; *A. Eichornii,* Claperide; *A. oculata*, Stein.

Spherical, translucent, vesicular or foamy, vesicles usually uniform; contractile vesicle single, large, active. Nucleus commonly obscured. Rays numerous, straight; length 1, 3 or 4 times the diameter of the body. Diameter of body, 40μ to 120μ; pseudopods, commonly 80μ to 160μ.

Hab.—In quiet waters with aquatic plants.

Actinophrys picta.

Similar to *A. sol*, but of a bright-green color, owing to the presence of chlorophyll mingled with the protoplasm. Diameter, 56μ to 105μ. Not common.

Hab.—Sphagnous swamps.

GENUS II.—HETEROPHRYS.

Animal resembling *Actinophrys*, but the body ordinarily enveloped with a thick stratum of protoplasm, defined by a granulated or thickly villous surface, and penetrated by pseudopodal rays.

Heterophrys myriapoda. — SYN. : *H. myriapoda*, Archer, Greeff : (?) *H. varians*, Schulze ; (?) *H. variabilis*, Greeff.

Body composed of a soft, usually spherical, granular mass of protoplasm, colorless at the surface, commonly bright-green within, due to chlorophyll corpuscules ; in some conditions with little or no color except such as is imparted by the food ; containing clear, colorless corpuscles, vacuoles, nuclei, and one or more contractile vesicles. With or without an exterior envelope of protoplasm. Pseudopods simple, granular rays. Diameter, $\frac{1}{380}$ to $\frac{1}{300}$ of an inch (Archer). [The range of this species does not seem to be well established, and it may include forms that are very variable in shape and appearance.]

GENUS III.—RAPHIDIOPHRYS.

Animals ordinarily associated in groups of variable number, closely aggregated or conjoined by isthmus-like bars. Individuals of Actinophryan form, consisting of a soft, spheroidal body of granular protoplasm, with oil-like molecules and variable proportions of clear, colorless or bright-green corpuscles, and a large, central nucleus. Exterior of the body invested with a thick layer of delicate, colorless protoplasm, extending in tapering processes

on the pseudopodal rays, and densely pervaded with
minute spicules, tangentially arranged. Pseudopodal
rays very long, numerous, straight, simple, finely
granulated.

Raphidiophrys viridis.

Single, or more frequently in closely aggregated groups
of variable number. Individuals green or colorless.
Spicules thickly distributed, tangentially arranged, extending outwardly on the bases of the pseudopodal rays,
comparatively coarse and slightly bent. Diameter about
$\frac{1}{300}$ of an inch (Archer), 90μ, Leidy.

Hab.—Ditches, rivers.

Raphidiophrys elegans.—Syn.: *A. oculata, sol,* Carter; *R. elegans,* H. and L., Leidy, Archer; *Sephærastrum conglobatum,* Greeff.

Single, or usually in groups of two or three dozen or
more, united by narrow bands. Individuals bright-green
from the presence of chlorophyll corpuscles, or colorless.
Spicules delicate, in the form of semicircles, tangentially
arranged, with their convexity directed toward the body
and the pseudopodals rays. Contractile vesicle changes
its position. Diameter, 32μ to 40μ; rays, 240μ; length
of semicircular spicules, 6μ.

Hab.—Springs and ponds among aquatic plants.

Genus IV.—Vampyrella.

Syn.: *Amœba,* Fresenius; *Vampyrella,* Cienkowski.

Animal usually Actinophrys-like, with a soft, spheroidal body, capable of amœboid variations of form;

composed of pale, colorless, granular protoplasm, with abundance of coloring matter, oil-like molecules, and vacuoles. Pseudopods as Actinophrys-like rays, Acineta-like rays, and digit-like, lobate, or wave-like expansions.

Vampyrella lateritia.—SYN. : *Amœba lateritia*, Fres., Cienk.; *V. spirogyræ*, Cienk., Häckel, H. and L., Archer.

Body brick or orange-red, with hyaline periphery, commonly spherical, but capable of much change of shape. Pseudopods Actinophrys-like rays, and also lobate extensions, together with Acineta-like rays [rays with heads, pin-like]. The pin-like rays are incessantly projected and withdrawn. The specimens observed by Prof. Leidy did not greatly change their shape. Diameter, 28.5μ to 83μ.

GENUS V.—DIPLOPHRYS.

SYN. : *Diplophrys*, Barker ; *Acanthocystis, Elæorhanis*, Greeff ; *Cystophrys*, Archer.

Animal minute, spheroidal; with a delicate homogeneous membranous investment, and a pair of oral orifices slightly lateral to the opposite poles. The interior, transparent, slightly granular protoplasm with a central nucleus, several pulsating vesicles, and usually a single, bright-yellow or red, oil-like globule. Pseudopods delicate, filamentous, and radiant in a tuft from both oral orifices. The young associated in groups, often of many individuals.

Diplophrys Archéri.—Syn. : *Diplophrys Archeri*, Barker, H. and L., Archer, Greeff, Schulze ; *Acanthocystis spinifera (?)* Greeff ; *Cystophrys oculea*, Archer ; *Elæorhanis cincta*, Greeff.

The only species; not observed by Prof. Leidy in the mature form. Diameter, 10μ to 20μ (Schulze). Those observed by Prof. Leidy, and placed by him in this group measured only 4μ to 5μ. They were transparent and each contained a bright, cherry-red, oil-like corpuscle.

Genus VI.—Actinosphærium.

Body spherical or oval, composed of finely granular protoplasm, enclosing a mass of delicate, polyhedral vesicles or vacuoles occupied by a clearer, hyaline protoplasm. The outer one or two layers of vacuoles more or less distinctly defined from the interior by greater size, translucency, and apparently by the intervention of a thicker film of granular protoplasm. Nuclei numerous and imbedded in the latter beneath the peripheral vacuoles. Contractile vesicles two, commonly opposite, in the peripheral layer. Rays numerous, tapering extensions of the granular protoplasm, including an axisthread, which starts beneath the peripheral vacuole layer.

Actinosphærium Eichornii.—Syn. : *Actinophrys Eichornii*, Ehr., Pritchard, and others ; *Actinophrys sol*, Kölliker ; *Actinosphærium Eichornii*, Stein, Greeff, H. and L., Schulze, Leidy.

Body transparent, colorless, usually with a single peripheral layer of the large vacuoles, which are deeper than broad ; or, in large and old individuals, sometimes

two peripheral layers of vacuoles of more uniform diameters.   The well-marked distinction between the outer
layer of vesicles and the inner mass, distinguishes this
from *Actinophrys*.   Diameter, 88μ to 400μ;   rays,
22μ.

Hab.—Ponds, ditches, lakes, among aquatic plants.

Genus VII.—Acanthocystis.

Syn. : *Trichoda,* Schrank ; *Actinophrys,* Ehr. ; *Acanthocystis,* Carter.

Animal Actinophrys-like in appearance.   Body spherical, soft, composed of finely granular protoplasm
mingled with bright-green and colorless corpuscles;
the former absent at times, also containing diffused
oil-globules, a central nucleus, vacuoles, and food in
balls.   Invested with numerous delicate, silicious rays,
implanted by minute basal disks and ending in a simple,
pointed or furcate extremity ; also giving off numerous
delicate, soft rays like *Actinophrys ;* further enveloped
by a layer of protoplasm, rising in pointed processes on
the rays, and pervaded by many exceedingly minute,
linear particles ; the enveloping layer sometimes absent.

Acanthocystis chœtophora. — Syn.: *Trichoda chœtophora,*
Schrank ; *Actinophrys viridis,* Duj., Perty, Pritchard, Mic. Dict.;
Acanthocystis turfacea, Carter, H. and L., Archer, Greeff ; *A. viridis,*
Greeff, Greenacher, Schneider, Leidy ; *A. pallida,* Greeff.

Body spherical, bright-green or colorless.   Nucleus
central, commonly obscured.   Silicious, or spiny, rays of
two kinds ; one long, strong, and acutely furcate ; the
other short, delicate, and widely furcate, sometimes absent.   Soft rays simple, granular, as long as, or longer

than the spinous rays. Exterior envelope of the body appearing like an atmosphere of exceedingly minute bacterium-like particles, sometimes absent. Diameter, 48μ to 100μ; length of furcate spines, 20μ to 60μ.

Hab.—Same as *Actinophrys* and *Actinosphærium.*

Acanthocystis ——— *?*

Spinous rays numerous, exceedingly delicate; emanating from lenticular disks at the surface of the body, and sharply pointed at the distal end. Enveloping layer of protoplasm finely granular, sometimes absent. Pseudopodal rays longer than the former. Diameter, 36μ to 48μ.

Hab.—Among aquatic plants in ponds and ditches.

Acanthocystis——— *?*

Body spherical, composed of a basis of granular protoplasm with a central nucleus, with green and colorless corpuscles, or colorless ones only. Spinous rays numerous, short, pin-like. Diameter, 39μ to 51μ.

Hab.—Among floating algæ.

Genus VIII.—Hyalolampe.

Syn. : *Hyalolampe*, Greeff ; *Pompholyxophrys*, Archer.

Animal spherical, composed of a finely granular protoplasmic mass, mingled with variable proportions of colored granules and vacuoles, with a central nucleus. Body invested with a thick layer of loosely coherent, minute, clear, silicious globules. Pseudopods few, radiant, exceedingly delicate, filamentous, not granular.

Hyalolampe fenestrata.—Syn.: *H. fenestrata*, Greeff, H. and L.; *Pompholyxophrys punicea*, Archer; *H. exigua*, H. and L.

Body more or less yellowish, brownish, or reddish. Investing silicious globules commonly in three layers. Diameter, 40μ to 80μ; silicious globules, 4μ.

Genus IX.—Clathrulina.

Syn.: *Clathrulina*, Cienk.; *Podosphæra*, Archer.

Animal provided with a spherical, latticed, silicious capsule, attached by a long, filiform stem to aquatic plants or other objects. Contents of the capsule a soft, Actinophrys-like body, with the same kind of pseudopodal rays which project through the openings of the capsule.

Clathrulina elegans.—Syn.: *C. elegans*, Cienk., Archer, Greeff, H. and L., Leidy; *Podosphæra Häckeliana*, Archer.

Capsule colorless, becoming yellow or brown with age; openings circular, or polygonal with rounded angles. When near maturity the sarcode contracts from the capsule. Body consists of soft, colorless, granular protoplasm, with scattered, oil-like molecules, numerous vacuoles and a central nucleus. Rays straight, mostly simple, somewhat furcate, long and numerous. Pedicle of variable length, attached by an expanded, lobate disk. While young the capsule is not obvious, and the pedicle is much thicker in proportion. Diameter of capsule, 30μ to 44μ [and more]; length of pedicle, 60μ to 260μ; thickness, 2μ, to 4μ.

Hab.—Ponds, ditches, swamps.

Order III.—Foraminifera.

The Foraminifera are almost exclusively marine, only a single well-defined genus, *Gromia*, is found in fresh-water.

Genus Gromia.

Animal spherical or oval, composed of granular protoplasm, with a large, central nucleus, and invested with a homogeneous, chitinoid membrane. Mouth terminal, and emitting copious streams of protoplasm, which flow around the body and extend into numerous pseudopodal rays, freely branching and anastomosing, so as to form an intricate net which exhibits an incessant flow of granules along the filaments both outward and inward.

Gromia terricola.

Body spherical or oval, pale-yellowish or cream-colored, more or less translucent. Shell chitinoid, thin, transparent, colorless or yellowish, with adhering sand and dirt. Interior protoplasm white by reflected light, pale-yellow by transmitted, granular, with fine oil-molecules, usually a few clear vacuoles, and a large, clear or pale, granular nucleus. Mouth obscure, emitting fine, granular protoplasm which breaks up into diverging and anastomosing streams. An incessant circulation of granules is to be observed along the filaments. Diameter, 112μ to 120μ; oval variety, 112μ long by 100μ broad.

Hab.—With moss, and in crevices of pavements in shaded places, in the City of Philadelphia

GENUS BIOMYXA.

Animal without a shell; initial form spherical, but incessantly changing, consisting of a glary, colorless, finely
granular protoplasm, which has the power of expanding
and extending itself in any direction, and of projecting
pseudopodal filaments, which freely branch and anasto-
mose. Granules circulate along the body and pseudopods ;
contractile vesicles numerous and minute, occurring in
both the body and in the pseudopods. Nucleus present
or absent. It is uncertain whether the animal which is
described under this genus is a Rhizopod, or the plas-
modium of a fungus, or whether it should be classed
among the Monera. It may be one of the naked Rhizopods, and in some cases looks like detached portions of
the sarcode of *Gromia*. A nucleated form has been
observed.

INDEX AND CHECK–LIST.

www.ingramcontent.com/pod-product-compliance
Lightning Source LLC
Chambersburg PA
CBHW021519090426
42739CB00007B/680